FAMOUS AIR FORCE FIGHTERS

GEORGE SULLIVAN

G. P. PUTNAM'S SONS ★ New York

Copyright © 1985 by George Sullivan.
All rights reserved.
This book, or parts thereof, may not be reproduced
in any form without permission in writing from the
publisher. Published in 1989 by G. P. Putnam's Sons,
a Division of The Putnam & Grosset Group,
200 Madison Avenue, New York, New York, 10016.
Originally published in 1985 by Dodd, Mead & Co., Inc.
Published simultaneously in Canada.
Printed in the United States of America.

Library of Congress Cataloging-in-Publication Data
Sullivan, George,   1927-
Famous Air Force fighters/George Sullivan.   p.   cm.
Reprint.   Originally: New York: Dodd, Mead, c1985.
SUMMARY: Traces the development of Air Force
aviation by examining specific types of fighter
planes.   1. Fighter planes—United States—
Juvenile literature.   2. Aeronautics, Military—
United States—History—Juvenile literature.
[1. Fighter planes—History.   2. Airplanes—
History.   3. United States. Air Force—
History.]   I. Title. UG1242.F5S918   1989
358.4'3'0973—dc19   89-3678   CIP   AC
ISBN 0-399-61253-X
10 9 8 7 6 5 4

INTRODUCTION

Orville and Wilbur Wright, a pair of bicycle mechanics from Dayton, Ohio, made the first successful flight in a motor-powered airplane at Kitty Hawk, North Carolina, on December 17, 1903. Although their rickety, open-cockpit biplane stayed in the air for only twelve seconds and covered merely 120 feet, it proved that man could build and fly a heavier-than-air craft.

Almost from the beginning, the Wrights tried to interest the government in their machine. Their efforts weren't successful until 1908. That year the newly founded Aeronautical Division of the U.S. Army Signal Corps, a forerunner of today's Air Force, called for the construction of a plane that was to be America's first military aircraft.

The Wrights built the machine and successfully tested it in 1909. It was then purchased by the Signal Corps.

Was the first military aircraft a bomber or a fighter? Neither, for such distinctions didn't exist at the time.

The earliest military aircraft, like the military balloons that had preceded them, were used mostly for gaining information about enemy troop movements and fortifications. If the Wrights' Military Flyer had been pressed into active service it probably would have been used for observation and reconnaissance.

Experiments and testing that led to the use of the airplane strictly as a fighter began about 1910. Then, in 1912, two years before World War I began, German plane-maker Anthony Fokker invented an "interrupter gear" that made it possible to fire a machine gun through the arc of a spinning propeller. Before Fokker's synchronized gun, gunners sometimes riddled the propellers off their own planes.

During World War I, most nations of the world, the U.S. among them, concentrated on the development of fighter-reconnaissance planes. This trend continued in the decade following the war.

The fighter aircraft of World War II are well known to many people. The fastest plane was the P-51 Mustang, built by North American Aviation. The Mustang could hit speeds of over 450 mph. But late in the war, the Germans introduced the Messerschmitt Me.262, the first jet fighter, whose speed easily surpassed that of the Mustang.

The United States put jet fighters into mass production in the postwar years, beginning with the F-80 Shooting Star. New types of wings and other structural improvements greatly increased the speed and maneuverability of fighter planes.

The decades of the 1970s and 1980s saw more advances in plane design. Space-age materials, such as titanium and other heat-resistant metals, began to be used in plane construction. Sophisticated electronic systems were introduced that are able to detect enemy aircraft and help the pilot seek out his target.

Today, the U.S. Air Force operates several different types of fighters. There are interceptors for defending against bomber attack. There are fighters for engaging enemy planes in air-to-air combat, and there are air-to-ground fighters for delivering bombs or missiles against ground targets.

This book profiles the planes that have had the greatest influence on fighter development. The aircraft appear in about the order each was introduced.

ACKNOWLEDGMENTS

The author is grateful to many individuals who helped him in the preparation of this book. Special thanks are due Maj. William H. Austin and Capt. Peter S. Meltzer, Air Force Office of Public Affairs, Arlington, Virginia; Robert Waller and Tom Cross, Defense Audio-Video Agency, Washington; Dana Bell, National Air and Space Museum, Washington, D.C.; Z. Joe Thornton and J. F. Isabel, General Dynamics; Harold Carr, Marilyn A. Phipps and Jack Wecker, The Boeing Company; Robert C. Ferguson, Lockheed-California Company; John F. Gulick, Fairchild-Republic; Francesca Kurti, TLC Custom Labs; Herb Field, Herb Field Studios; and Bill Sullivan.

CONTENTS

In early aircraft purchased by the military, engines were mounted behind the wing, and served to "push" the plane through the air.

CURTISS PUSHER

The United States Air Force, the organization that was to become the most powerful military force in history, got started in 1907. On August 1 of that year, the U.S. Army established within the Signal Corps an Aeronautical Division which was made responsible for "all matters pertaining to military ballooning, air machines, and kindred subjects."

The early aircraft purchased by the Aeronautical Division were not much of an advance over the Wright Brothers' plane flown at Kitty Hawk. Like the Wrights' machine, they were of the "pusher" type. That is, the engine was mounted behind the pilot, and its propeller pushed the plane through the air. (In later planes, the engine would be mounted at the front of the aircraft, and the propeller would pull rather than push.)

One of these early planes was the Curtiss Pusher, developed by Glenn H. Curtiss, a noted aviation pioneer. A biplane, the Curtiss machine was a fragile-looking craft, made of wood, wire, and cotton fabric. The tail and wing surfaces were linked by bamboo poles, which were strong yet light. Taping the bamboo at intervals prevented splintering.

A bit less than 26 feet in length, the Curtiss airplane had a nose section that resembled a box kite and a big rudder at the tail. The pilot's seat was in the open, fixed to the front edge of the lower wing.

During this period, Aeronautical Division pilots sometimes experimented with these airplanes, showing the different uses to which they might be put. Aviators leaned out of cockpits to take serial photographs and demonstrated the advantages of sending two-way telegraph messages.

The first use of an airplane as a platform for a gun dates to this time. On August 20, 1910, at the old Sheepshead Bay Race Track in Brooklyn, New York, Glenn Curtiss eased one of his planes into the summer sky. Seated next to him was Lt. Jacob E. Fickel. Fickel was armed with a rifle. While Curtiss circled at an altitude of 100 feet, Fickel fired two bullets into a small target.

It had been believed that the recoil created when firing a gun from an airplane would rip the flimsy machine to pieces. Curtiss and Fickel disproved that theory.

About two years later, in June, 1912, Capt. Charles Chandler and Lt. Thomas Milling fired a Lewis machine gun from a plane. Military leaders began to realize that they had devised a devastating weapon. Out of these primitive beginnings, the first fighter planes began to evolve.

Other Data (Model D)
Wingspan: 26 ft., 3 in.
Length: 25 ft., 6 in.
Power Plant: One 8-cylinder, 60-80-hp Curtiss
Loaded Weight: 700 lb.
Maximum Speed: 70 mph

CURTISS SCHOOL of AVIATION

Buffalo, N. Y.   Miami, Fla.   Hammondsport, N. Y.
Newport News, Va.   San Diego, Cal.

Under Aviation Section, United States Army, Supervision

Aviation schools featuring Curtiss Jennies were hailed in this World War I recruiting poster.

CURTISS JN

During World War I, the dual-cockpit Curtiss JN, known as the Jenny, was the most widely used plane in the United States. While chiefly a training plane, it did see brief but not so glorious action service in a military foray into Mexico in 1916.

The Jenny dates to 1914, only eleven years after the Wright Brothers had first flown at Kitty Hawk. The plane was produced by the Curtiss Aeroplane and Motor Co. in response to a request from the U.S. Army for a training plane in which to train aviators.

The Curtiss Company hired B. D. Thomas of Great Britain's Sopwith Aviation to design the plane. His JN-1, as it was called, was evaluated by the U.S. Army and Navy, and certain improvements were requested. These were included in the JN-2, ten of which were ordered by the Army.

At the time the Aviation Section of the Army's Signal Corps was taking delivery of the JNs, World War I in Europe had been underway for about a year. Military leaders were using planes for scouting bombing missions and photo-mapping. They also assisted the artillery by directing the fall of shells. Some served as fighter planes and carried machine guns that fired through the propeller.

The twenty-nine officers, 155 enlisted men, and eight JNs that made up the Aviation Section were sent to Fort Sill, Oklahoma. While there, they were to see what they could accomplish working with artillery units.

Their assignment did not last long. On March 9, 1916, the Mexican revolutionist Pancho Villa and several hundred armed and mounted men swept into the little town of Columbus, New Mexico. In the street fighting that followed, seventeen Americans were killed. The U.S. government ordered Gen. John Pershing to lead an expedition into Mexico to bring back Villa.

Pershing asked for the assistance of the men and planes of the Aviation Section. But the JNs were not fit for military service. As armament, some of the pilots carried pistols. Two fliers had .22-caliber rifles. They would later be supplied with machine guns. For bombs, they were given three-inch shells intended for the artillery. None of the pilots knew how to use them.

The Army ordered the planes from Columbus to Casas Grandes in Mexico. It was an order the JNs were not able to carry out. Engine trouble forced one plane to return to Columbus. Three planes became lost; two landed successfully but a third cracked up. The remaining four were forced to make emergency landings.

Despite their dismal showing in Mexico, the Jennies went on to write a brilliant chapter in American aviation history. Advanced models of the plane were built by the thousands. More than 5,500 JN-4s were turned out. After World War I and throughout much of the 1920s, many of these Jennies stayed active as flying-circus and barnstorming aircraft.

Other Data (Model: JN-3)
Wingspan: 43 ft., 7⅜ in.
Length: 27 ft., 4 in.
Power Plant: One 90-hp water-cooled Curtiss OX-5
Takeoff Weight: 2,130 lb.
Maximum Speed: 75 mph at sea level

After World War I, the Jenny was often the plane used by barnstormers and acrobats.

CURTISS P-6

The sleek and handsome Curtiss P-6 was called the "most beautiful fighter plane ever built." Constructed of metal tubing instead of wood and fitted with one of the most powerful engines available at the time, the P-6 was the first American military plane capable of exceeding 200 mph in level flight.

The plane came to the attention of the Air Service in 1923, when, carrying the designation PW-8, it was pitted in a dramatic race against the sun across the nation. Lt. Russell Maughan climbed into the fighter at Mitchel Field, Long Island, shortly before dawn on the morning of June 24, 1924. He roared down the runway and into the air, and set down to refuel at Dayton, Ohio, four hours later. Other refueling stops were made at St. Joseph, Missouri; North Platte, Nebraska; Casper, Wyoming; and Salduro, Utah.

Curtiss P-6E, introduced in the early 1930s, was favorite of Army fliers of the day.

Curtiss P-6Es, piloted by members of the 17th Pursuit Squadron, fly in formation near Selfridge Field, Michigan, in 1932.

Maughan touched down at Crissy Field in San Francisco just as the late summer sun was disappearing over the Pacific Ocean. "Well, I had a wonderful time," Maughan told the big crowd that had awaited him.

Maughan and his Curtiss, in the air for 18 hours and 20 minutes, had averaged 156 mph. "This is not a circus stunt," an Air Service officer proclaimed. "It is a test of what the United States aviation services may someday be called upon to do.

"It is an attempt to show that Army fliers, given the proper equipment, can be sent from any section of the country to any other section, should the emergency arise."

So impressed was the Air Service with Maughan's feat, it ordered twenty-five PW-8s.

In 1925, when the Air Service changed its classification system, the PW-8 became the P-1. In the years that followed, the aircraft went through a number of design changes, from P-1 through P-2, P-3, P-5, and P-6.

The P-6E, introduced in 1932, was the most noted of all models. Highly maneuverable, it was a favorite of pilots everywhere.

It carried two synchronized machine guns— one .30-caliber and one .50-caliber. A still later model, the P-6H, mounted six machine guns, the most carried by any fighter until World War II.

Other Data (Model: P-6)
Wingspan: 31 ft., 6 in.
Length: 23 ft., 2 in.
Power Plant: One 600-hp liquid-cooled Curtiss
    Conqueror
Loaded Weight: 3,436 lb.
Maximum Speed: 197 mph

BOEING P-12

During the period between World War I and World War II, the P-12 was perhaps the best known of all fighter aircraft. A short and stubby biplane with a powerful engine, the P-12 saw service with the U.S. Navy as well as with the Army Air Corps.

Although the ship never flew in combat, the P-12 was involved in a turbulent chapter in the history of military aviation. Under an order issued by President Franklin D. Roosevelt early in 1934, the Air Corps was forced to fly the United States mail for a short period when contracts with commercial airlines were cancelled.

Most Army planes of the day were not equipped for the chore. None had navigation lights or landing lights. Radios were unreliable. Yet pilots were expected to fly over unfamiliar terrain at night.

One pilot, Lt. C. R. Springer, took off in his P-12 loaded with mail, but angrily returned to his field at Cleveland about fifteen minutes later. As Springer taxied his plane to a halt, a mechanic came running out onto the field to find out what was wrong. Springer was fuming. "Get me a flashlight," he shouted, "so I can find my way out of this damned town."

A pilot was killed when thick clouds enveloped his plane and his radio and altimeter failed. Another pilot became lost in fog over Maryland and

A compact little biplane, the P-12 was perhaps the best known of all aircraft in the years between World Wars I and II.

Its 500-hp engine could whisk the P-12 along at close to 200 mph.

circled a small town until local residents came out and lighted a level field with automobile headlights.

The Air Corps was not permitted to give up its mail-carrying mission until late in 1934. By that time, there had been sixty-six accidents that had claimed the lives of twelve men.

The decade ahead was to demand an Air Force meant for far greater tasks than delivering air mail. In 1935, Adolph Hitler announced that German youth were to be drafted for military service. By 1937, an all-out war was raging between China and Japan. Hitler launched his conquest of Europe by attacking Poland in 1939.

For its fighter planes, the United States could no longer relay on chunky little biplanes, poorly equipped. A new era was at hand.

Other Data (Model: P-12E)
Wingspan: 30 ft.
Length: 20 ft., 3 in.
Power Plant: One 500-hp air-cooled Pratt & Whitney Wasp
Loaded Weight: 2,690 lb.
Maximum Speed: 189 mph at 7,000 ft.

BOEING P-26

Until the introduction of Boeing's P-26, fighter planes were invariably biplanes. The P-26, a high-performance, all-metal monoplane, marked a turning point.

While the P-26 represented an important breakthrough in design, it had several properties common to its predecessors—an open cockpit, fixed landing gear, and external wing bracing. It would be the last of the Army's pursuit planes to have these features.

The P-26 was powered by a 600-hp, nine-cylinder Pratt & Whitney air-cooled Wasp engine. The plane's armament consisted of either two .30-caliber machine guns or one .30-caliber and one .50-caliber machine gun. In either case, the guns were synchronized to fire through the propeller. Two 100-pound or five 30-pound bombs could be carried in the plane's wing racks.

Overall, the P-26 had a chunky appearance. Pilots referred to it as the "pea-shooter."

The design project that was to result in the P-26 began in January, 1932. An experimental model of the plane flew on March 20 of the same year. The success of flight tests convinced the Army to order 111 P-26As in January, 1933. Later, twenty-four B and C models were ordered, bringing the total production to 135 aircraft.

Between the years 1932 and 1934, the P-26 set military records for both speed and altitude. Its maximum speed was 234 mph at 7,500 feet.

Leather-helmeted P-26 pilots pose with the planes.

But the P-26 was not all that the Army was seeking. Bomber technology had been developing so rapidly that most bombers were faster than the pursuit planes that were supposed to intercept them. Nevertheless, the P-26 served as the nation's first line of air defense from the mid-to-late 1930s. It was replaced by the faster, more-advanced Republic Seversky P-35 and the Curtiss P-36.

When the P-26 was removed from service, many of the planes were at overseas bases. They were sold to the countries where they happened to be serving. China, the Philippines, Spain, and Panama were among the nations that purchased them.

A final chapter in the story of the P-26 was written in December, 1941, when World War II erupted in the Pacific, with the Japanese attacking Pearl Harbor and other American bases at Manila and Singapore. The hand-me-down P-26s with the Philippine Air Force fought gallant but futile battles against the much more advanced and numerous Japanese bombers and fighters.

Other Data (Model: P-26A)
Wingspan: 27 ft., 11 in.
Length: 23 ft., 7 in.
Power Plant: One 600-hp air-cooled Pratt & Whitney Wasp
Loaded Weight: 2,955 lb.
Maximum Speed: 234 mph

During early 1930s, U.S. Army ordered a total of 136 P-26s. This is Boeing Company's production line.

CURTISS P-36

The Curtiss P-36 is noted for two important breakthroughs: It (along with the Seversky P-35) was the first American-built, single-seat fighter to be equipped with a retractable landing gear and the first to offer an enclosed cockpit.

Thanks to these and other innovations, the P-36 gave the United States an advantage in fighter plane technology during the 1930s, but only for a

In anticipation of the war that was soon to come, this P-36A, photographed in 1939, wears camouflage.

A squadron of Curtiss P-36As practices formation flying.

short period. By 1939, the P-36 was already out of date, unable to perform on the same level with Great Britain's Hawker Hurricane and Supermarine Spitfire and Germany's Messerschmitt Me. 109.

Design and development work on the plane that was to become the P-36 began during November, 1934, and continued for more than two years. The Army Air Corps ordered 210 P-36As on July 7, 1937. Delivery of these began in 1938.

Well-designed and able to perform every task it was assigned, the P-36 was happily received by pilots of the day. But in terms of speed and range and other features, the P-36 was soon surpassed by the Bell P-38 and Curtiss' own P-40.

On the morning of December 7, 1941, when the Japanese attacked Pearl Harbor, some thirty-nine P-36As were in Hawaii. Four managed to get into the air and shoot down two Japanese bombers.

One of the P-36 pilots, Lt. John L. Dains, was shot down under tragic circumstances. Over Scho-

field Barracks, American infantrymen fired Springfield rifles, Browning automatic rifles, and Colt pistols at anything in the sky. Blasted by this fire, Dains crashed to his death.

While the P-36 was pressed into service in the opening stages of the war against Japan, the plane was soon assigned a role as a trainer. A more powerful version of the P-36, designated the Hawk 75, was supplied to the French air force. These planes were transferred to Great Britain after the fall of France. This same model also served with the air force of Norway.

Other Data (Model: P-36C)
Wingspan: 37 ft., 4 in.
Length: 28 ft., 10 in.
Power Plant: One 1,200-hp Pratt & Whitney
    Twin Wasp
Loaded Weight: 6,010 lb.
Maximum Speed: 311 mph at 10,000 ft.

From a standpoint of both design and performance, the P-38 Lightning represented a great leap forward.

LOCKHEED P-38 LIGHTNING

Air Force historians call the Lockheed P-38 the first "great" American fighter. To German pilots of World War II, it was the "fork-tailed devil." Japanese airmen hated and feared it more than any other plane.

The P-38 was designed in 1937 as a long-range tactical fighter. But its development was delayed because military strategists believed that American heavy bombers on long missions would be perfectly capable of defending themselves, and no escorting fighter planes would be necessary. When this theory proved tragically wrong, P-38s were rushed into production and sent to Europe in big numbers.

18

The P-38 had none of the shortcomings of the later P-39 and or P-40. It achieved speeds of up to 414 mph at 25,000 feet. It had spectacular diving speed. In September, 1942, Lt. Col. Cass Hough took a P-38 to 43,000 feet and dove down to 25,000 feet before leveling off. During the dive, the needle on Hough's air speed indicator hit 780 mph.

The P-38 was the first American plane to shoot down a German aircraft. The victim was a FW-200 Condor which came under Lightning attack while spotting ships for German submarines near Iceland in August, 1942. The Lightning's first large-scale use was in North Africa that November.

In time, the P-38s chalked up hundreds of victories over German aircraft. But it was the Pacific where the plane earned its greatest fame, shooting down more Japanese aircraft than any other Allied fighter.

Two American P-38 pilots must be mentioned. One, Maj. Richard Bong, downed all forty of his Japanese victims while at the controls of a Lightning. The other Lightning pilot, Maj. Thomas McGuire, had thirty-eight Japanese kills.

Almost 10,000 P-38s were built by Lockheed between 1940 and 1945. While the plane usually served as a fighter or light bomber, it was also the most widely used photoreconnaissance aircraft of World War II.

Other Data (Model: P-38L)
Wingspan: 52 ft.
Length: 37 ft., 10 in.
Power Plant: Two 1,425-hp liquid-cooled Allisons
Loaded Weight: 17,500 lb.
Maximum Speed: 414 mph at 25,000 ft.

Enemy pilots hated and feared the P-38 Lightning.

Powerful 37-mm cannon
juts from nose of Bell P-39.

BELL P-39 AIRACOBRA

The P-39 Airacobra was a plane designed around a big gun, the gun being a 37-mm cannon.

The engine was gotten out of the way by placing it behind the cockpit. Because the engine was so far to the rear, an unusual tricycle landing gear was necessary so the plane would be able to stay properly balanced on landings and takeoffs.

Besides the big gun, the P-39 was armed with four .50-caliber machine guns, two in the nose that fired through the propeller, and two in the wing. The plane also carried a 500-pound bomb.

The Air Corps ordered a test model of the P-39 on October 7, 1937. Several design changes followed before the aircraft went into full production in August, 1939.

The P-39 had excellent speed at low altitude

and, of course, tremendous firepower. It was also capable of absorbing heavy punishment from enemy fire.

But there were problems with the plane. The P-39 had no supercharger, not because of any technical problems, but because the Army thought it to be unnecessary. Not having a supercharger, which pumped air into the engine, enabling it to function at high altitudes, was a serious failing.

Here's how one pilot described the P-39 in flight: "Upon climbing through 12,000 feet, you felt as if you had hit a brick wall, and then the climb from 12,000 feet to 25,000 feet was at a snail's pace."

Not only was climbing speed reduced, but, because of its stubby wings, the plane had little maneuverability.

When confronted by a Zero, Japan's foremost fighter, the P-39 pilot had to try either to lure the enemy plane to a low altitude, where they could battle on even terms, or swoop down on the Zero from a high altitude, a "dive for life," as one P-39 pilot called it.

Summing up, another pilot said: "The P-39 was virtually worthless above 15,000 feet, and this was at a time when enemy planes were routinely flying at 35,000 to 40,000 feet."

Of the 9,558 P-39s produced during World War II, 4,773 were sent to the Soviet Union. There they won high praise. Russian pilots used the P-39 and its big gun with deadly effect against German tanks and other ground targets. They called the P-39 the best low-altitude fighter of the war.

Other Data (Model: P-39Q)
Wingspan: 34 ft.
Length: 30 ft., 2 in.
Power Plant: One 1,200-hp liquid-cooled Allison
Loaded Weight: 8,300 lb.
Maximum Speed: 385 mph at 11,000 ft.

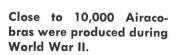

Close to 10,000 Airacobras were produced during World War II.

Curtiss P-40 Warhawks near Hawaii in August, 1941, a few months before the outbreak of World War II.

CURTISS P-40 WARHAWK

The P-40 saw action in more places than any other World War II fighter. It was at Pearl Harbor and the Philippines when the Japanese struck. It fought in every theater of operations, including North Africa and China. The air forces of no fewer than twenty nations flew the P-40.

Nevertheless, the P-40 was a controversial ship.

Like the P-39, it lacked a supercharger, which put the plane at a disadvantage at high altitudes where enemy planes were often faster and more maneuvarable.

After being tested in May, 1939, in competition with other pursuit aircraft, the P-40A was put into production. A total of 524 P-40As were built.

Design changes for the P-40B included armor protection for the pilot. And the wing firepower was doubled, from two .30-caliber machine guns to

Flying Tigers painted their P-40s with sharks'-teeth emblems.

four of them. In addition, there were two .50-caliber machine guns mounted on the engine cowling.

With the P-40C, Curtiss introduced self-sealing gas tanks. In later models, the plane's top speed was boosted to around 380 mph at 10,500 feet.

On December 7, 1941, a handful of P-40s managed to get into the air at Pearl Harbor and bring down a few of the attacking Japanese aircraft. But the P-40 earned its greatest fame in China. It was the plane flown by the American Volunteer Group of the Chinese Air Force, the "Flying Tigers," as they were called. They went into combat two weeks after Pearl Harbor.

When the American pilots and ground-crew members in China heard that the Japanese feared sharks, they painted their P-40s with sharks' teeth emblems on the nose. They were going to call the planes "Tiger Sharks," but "Flying Tigers" was the name that became popular.

The Flying Tigers were based at Kunming in China. There were never more than seventy pilots in the group. Although they usually went into action against great odds, they were almost always successful. One reason for this was because the Flying Tigers fought in two-plane teams. One member of the team always flew at a high altitude, keeping watch over his partner. If the partner came under attack, the other plane flew down to join in. Before the group was disbanded in 1942, Flying Tiger P-40s shot down 286 Japanese air-

P-40 trainers from Randolph Field, Texas

craft while suffering only eight losses.

American factories turned out P-40s for six years. More than 14,000 were built. The fastest model was the XP-40Q, built in 1945. It could travel at a speed of 422 mph. But by 1945, World War II was winding down, and the XP-40Q never went into full production.

Other Data (Model: P-40F)
Wingspan: 37 ft., 4 in.
Length: 33 ft., 4 in.
Power Plant: One 1,300-hp liquid-cooled
    Rolls Royce Merlin
Loaded Weight: 9,870 lb.
Maximum Speed: 365 mph

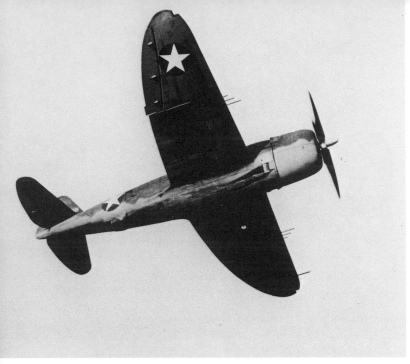

Its stubby body earned the P-47 Thunderbolt the nickname of the "flying milk bottle."

REPUBLIC P-47 THUNDERBOLT

Republic's P-47 was a rough, tough fighting plane. Known as the "flying milk bottle" because of its shape, and also nicknamed the "Jug," the P-47 could outdive any fighter and became well known for its ability to survive battle damage.

The Thunderbolt was originally designed for duty in escorting B-17 Flying Fortresses and B-24 Liberators on bombing missions over Europe. But the plane did not have the ability to stay with the bombers much beyond the Belgian border. The role of escort eventually went to the P-51 Mustang.

The experimental model of the P-47 was first flown on May 6, 1941. It turned in a speed of 412 mph.

Although the plane was a speedster, British pilots grinned when they saw the P-47 for the first time. They didn't believe that the beefy Thunderbolt would have much of a chance against the zippy German fighters.

But the Thunderbolt quickly showed that it could take care of itself. Although it was much heavier than any other single-engine fighter, it could climb to 15,000 feet in six minutes, thanks to its unusual tail-mounted supercharger. It handled beautifully at altitudes above 30,000 feet, and from there could dive down at an airspeed of just over 500 mph.

The Thunderbolt was a very durable plane. Once, on a ground-strafing mission, a P-47 had nine of its fourteen cylinders shot away, yet the pilot still managed to get back to his base. Another time, a Thunderbolt rammed into a tall steel tower. Although the collision ripped four feet of the plane's right wing, it limped safely back home.

American aces (an ace is a combat pilot who has downed five or more enemy planes) in Europe saw their scores mount, thanks to the Thunderbolt. The most noted of the P-47 pilots was Lt. Col. Francis

Gabreski with thirty-one victories.

The P-47 Thunderbolt earned its greatest praise at low altitudes, shooting up German airfields, and railyards, and other ground targets. From March, 1943, when it went on active duty, until the war's end in August, 1945, P-47s flew on every front, destroying over 7,000 aircraft on the ground and in the air.

Altogether, 15,570 Thunderbolts were produced.

The last was phased out of service in 1955.

Other Data (Model: P-47D)
Wingspan: 40 ft., 9 in.
Length: 36 ft., 1 in.
Power Plant: One 2,000-hp air-cooled Pratt & Whitney Double Wasp
Loaded Weight: 14,600 lb.
Maximum Speed: 429 mph

The P-47N, the long-range model of the Thunderbolt

Very fast and with enormous range, the Mustang was favorite of World War II fighter pilots.

NORTH AMERICAN P-51 MUSTANG

What was the best Allied fighter plane of World War II? A pilot in the Royal Air Force would surely name the Spitfire, the aircraft credited with winning the Battle of Britain. American pilots had their own favorite—the P-51 Mustang.

The Mustang was quick and fast and had a greater cruising range than any other fighter in the European Theater of Operations. It is said that when German Field Marshal Hermann Goering saw Mustangs in the sky over Berlin he admitted for the first time that Germany could no longer win the war.

In April, 1940, the British Purchasing Company asked North American Aviation to build a fighter plane to replace the P-40. The British said the new ship would have to be ready in the seemingly impossible time of 120 days. North American delivered the plane in 117 days.

Called the XP-51, the new plane was first flown in October, 1940. The first production models were delivered the following year. It was RAF pilots who christened the P-51A the Mustang.

This early model was a good plane but not a great one. It lacked power at high altitudes, and thus was no match for Germany's powerful Messerschmitt Me.109. The P-51A was given a role as a low-altitude fighter and a photoreconnaissance plane.

At about the same time the P-51A was beginning active service, the first B-17 Flying Fortresses were arriving in England from the United States. Air Force strategists planned to use the B-17s for the daylight bombing of Germany. They asked the RAF to provide fighters to escort the bombers to their German targets. The RAF commanders threw up their hands. "Our fighters don't have the range," they said.

Indeed, it was true. The Spitfire, although a wonderfully maneuverable plane, carried only 85 Imperial gallons (106 U.S. gallons) of fuel. The plane had to do its fighting within a hundred miles of home.

A solution to the problem was at hand, however. In 1942, the British developed the Merlin 61, an advanced Rolls Royce engine with a powerful

The Merlin 61, an advanced Rolls Royce engine, enabled the P-51 to perform brilliantly at high altitudes.

supercharger that cut in at about 20,000 feet, providing high performance all the way to 40,000 feet and even beyond.

When a Merlin-equipped Mustang, the P-51B, was flight-tested at Wright Field in Dayton, Ohio, it performed brilliantly at high altitudes. Its speed was also much improved, increasing to 442 mph. (It had been 390 mph.)

Delivery of the P-51B to the Eighth Air Force in England began on December 1, 1943. These

Mustangs flew their first missions twelve days later.

With the introduction of the P-51B, precision bombing of European targets entered a new and much more aggressive phase. Fitted with wing fuel tanks, called "drop" tanks because they could be "dropped" by the pilot after being emptied, the P-51 could range over a thousand miles from its base, far enough to escort B-17 and B-24 bombers all the way to Berlin and back.

Pilots raved about the P-51. It was comfortable and relatively roomy, a pleasure to fly. It had plenty of speed, power, and range. It could out-dive and outrun the Me.109. As a long-range escort fighter, it had no equal.

In clashes with the *Luftwaffe*, the German Air Force, the Mustang achieved an outstanding record—seven enemy planes destroyed for every P-51 lost in combat. During March and April of 1944, one Mustang group blasted 235 German airplanes out of the sky.

The P-51 also saw service in the Pacific. Based on Iwo Jima, a tiny volcanic island south of the Japanese mainland, P-51s escorted B-29 Superfortresses on their bombing runs to Tokyo, Yokohama, Kobe, Nagoya, and other Japanese cities, cities more than a thousand miles away.

North American experimented with a Twin Mustang for escorting bombers on long-range missions. The Twin Mustang, designated the P-82, was achieved by putting two P-51 fuselages together with a single wing. The plane that resulted

A total of 14,817 Mustangs were built during World War II.

P-51 Mustangs of the Alaskan Air Command above the clouds over rugged Alaskan terrain.

resembled the P-38. World War II ended before the P-82 went into full production. Only about twenty were built.

The P-51 holds the distinction of being one of the few aircraft to come into existence during the years of World War II and to see wide-scale service. A total of 14,817 Mustangs were built.

After World War II, the P-51 was not retired, but went on to serve in Korea, although the plane's designation was changed to F-51. The airframe design went on to become the F-51D, a U.S. tactical support aircraft of the 1960s and civilian sport aircraft.

Other Data (Model: P-51D)
Wingspan: 37 ft.
Length: 32 ft., 3 in.
Power Plant: One 1,450-hp Rolls Royce Merlin
Loaded Weight: 10,100 lb.
Maximum Speed: 437 mph

NORTHROP P-61 BLACK WIDOW

Big, black, and deadly, the P-61 Black Widow was the first Air Force plane designed from the landing gear up as a night fighter. It earned a reputation as the best night fighter of World War II, frequently bewildering enemy aircraft with its uncanny radar-directed attacks in total darkness. The Black Widow also played an important role as a rescue plane, often guiding pilots home who were lost over the ocean at night.

Northrop began work on the P-61 in 1940, basing its initial designs on what the Royal Air Force had learned in night bombing raids on occupied Europe. This experience dictated that a night fighter should have plenty of endurance, the most advanced radar available, and the heaviest possible armor and armament.

The first prototype for the Black Widow flew in May, 1942. The first production models became available late in 1943.

Three men—a pilot, radar operator, and gunner—made up the crew of the P-61. The ship was armed with four .50-caliber machine guns and four 20-mm cannons. It could carry either four 1,600-pound bombs or 300-gallon drop tanks under its wings.

During the early months of 1944, the P-61 went on active duty with fighter groups in the South Pacific. Japanese bombers from bases on the island

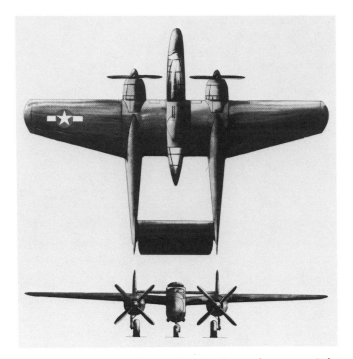

The first Air Force plane designed purely as a night fighter, the P-61 saw action in both Europe and the Pacific during World War II.

of Iwo Jima had been attacking B-29 airfields in the Mariana Islands. Black Widows solved this problem, seeking out the enemy before they struck, then destroying them with their cannons and machine guns.

Black Widows were in service in Europe by July, 1944. In their first engagement, they shot down four German bombers. Black Widows were also capable of destroying V-1 "flying bombs."

By the end of 1945, when World War II had ended, 706 P-61s had been built. Most of these were retired, but 36 Black Widows were converted for use as reconnaissance planes. Redesignated the RF-61C, and nicknamed the "Reporter," this plane continued in service until 1952.

Other Data (Model: P-61B)
Wingspan: 66 ft.
Length: 49 ft., 7 in.
Power Plant: Two 2,000-hp Pratt & Whitney Double Wasps
Loaded Weight: 29,700 lb.
Maximum Speed: 366 mph at 20,000 ft.

The P-61 Black Widow carried a crew of three—a pilot, radar operator, and gunner.

Designed and tested during final stages of World War II,
the F-80 Shooting Star was the Air Force's first jet fighter.

LOCKHEED F-80 SHOOTING STAR

On January 8, 1944, the day the XP-80, the prototype of the F-80 Shooting Star, took wing for the first time, every other airplane in the Air Force became obsolete. The Shooting Star was much more than simply a new fighter; it was a jet fighter, the first of a new breed that was to vault aviation into the supersonic age.

The XP-80 was designed, built, and tested during World War II. Toward the end of the war, in 1944, Germany had introduced the Messerschmitt Me.262 Schwalbe (Swallow), a jet fighter. The Me.262 scored one deadly victory after another over American B-17s and B-24s, signaling the end of the era of propeller-driven bombers. The Shooting Star was meant to answer the challenge of the German plane.

The first Shooting Star was designed and built in the record time of 143 days. Great secrecy cloaked the project. Some Lockheed employees ate and slept in the hangar where the plane was built until the job was done. The F-80 was test-flown on January 8, 1944.

The F-80 was a light plane, relatively speaking, weighing 12,744 pounds. It handled beautifully. It boasted a cruising speed of 439 mph and a maximum speed of 580 mph, some one hundred miles an hour faster than the best of the World War II fighters (and 40 mph faster than the Messerschmitt Me.262).

In 1947, the F-80 set world's speed record of 623.8 mph.

After World War II, updated models of the Shooting Star set one speed record after another. The plane's most stunning achievement came on June 19, 1947, when a Shooting Star whooshed through the sky at a record 623.8 mph. That marked the first time in twenty-four years that the United States had held the world's speed record,

While the F-80 was designed for war, it seemed it would never see combat. Then, in 1950, North Korea attacked South Korea, and United Nations forces, made up partly of American units, went to the aid of the South Koreans. All available aircraft, F-80s included, were sent to the battle zone.

As South Korea was aided by the UN, so North Korea was backed by Communist China. The Chinese Air Force had the use of Russian-built MiG-15 swept-wing fighters. (The term MiG is derived from the first letters of the last names of the plane's designers, Artem *Mi*koyan and Mikhail *G*urevich.)

F-80 served as Air Force's frontline fighter through 1960s and into 1970s.

On November 8, 1950, F-51s and F-80s were flying escort for seventy B-29s sent to bomb a pair of bridges spanning the Yalu River that separates North Korea and China. American fighter pilots saw a handful of MiGs take to the air from a field on the other side of the river, climb in a hurry to 30,000 feet, then whip down to attack the bombers. The F-80s turned to meet the attack head-on.

The MiGs made one firing pass without doing any damage, then scampered back across the Yalu. American planes were not permitted to go beyond the river. But one of the Russian jets was caught in a shallow dive by Lt. Russell J. Brown, whose F-80 closed the distance before the MiG could reach its sanctuary. Brown's six .50-caliber machine guns zeroed in on the MiG and it went down trailing smoke to crash on the river bank. It was the first all-jet air battle in history. It had taken less than thirty seconds.

Generally, the F-80 was outclassed by the MiG-15, which was faster and had a higher rate of climb. As a ground-attack plane, however, the F-80 was unsurpassed. Its six .50-caliber machine guns in the wings gave it the firepower needed for strafing trains, vehicles, and gun positions.

The plane also got high marks as a dive bomber. It carried a 1,000-pound bomb under each wing.

The last F-80 came off the production line in

Formation of F-80 Shooting Stars during air show in Miami, Florida, in 1949

1950. During a six-and-one-half-year period, 1,732 Shooting Stars were built. The plane continued to serve as a frontline fighter, not only for the U.S. Air Force, but for the U.S. Navy and five South American nations until the early 1970s.

By that time, the F-80 had achieved some notable firsts. It was the first American jet fighter to fly the Atlantic Ocean, and the first jet to become an Air Force standby.

A dual-control tandem-seat version of the F-80, known as the T-33, became the most famous of all jet trainers. During the 1950s, approximately 90 percent of the free world's pilots trained in the T-33.

Other Data (Model: F-80C)
Wingspan: 38 ft., 10 in.
Length: 34 ft., 6 in.
Power Plant: One 5,400-lb.-thrust Allison turbojet
Loaded Weight: 15,336 lb.
Maximum Speed: 594 mph

A Lockheed F-80 in a rocket-assisted takeoff.

REPUBLIC F-84 THUNDERJET

Like the F-80 Shooting Star, the F-84 Thunderjet did an exceptional job of providing ground support during the Korean War. Many times F-84s prevented disaster for South Korean, American, and other United Nations forces, which often faced overwhelming numbers of the enemy.

The first prototypes of the F-84 were ordered early in 1945. One of these was flown on February 28, 1946. The same year, a second prototype established a U.S. national speed record of 611 mph.

During the early stages of the Korean War, the first combat missions were flown by F-51 Mustangs and F-80 Shooting Stars. Both of these planes were also used to escort B-29 bombers. When F-84 Thunderjets began arriving in Korea, the plane took over both of these roles.

The F-84 was forty miles an hour faster than the F-80, capable of carrying a much heavier bomb load and had a greater range. It became the workhorse plane of the Korean War, flying more sorties and dropping more bombs than any other fighter-bomber.

But strictly as a fighter plane, the F-84 was not the equal of the Soviet-built MiG-15. Above 20,000 feet, the F-84 could not turn as quickly or as tightly as the MiG-15, and its lack of speed when compared to that of the Russian fighter put it at a serious disadvantage. Only their superior training and flying skills enabled F-84 pilots to deal with the Soviet aircraft.

The F-84 was the last subsonic, straight-wing fighter to see service with the Air Force. However, the plane was later modified so as to include swept-back wings. This model first flew in June, 1950. It was known as the F-84F Thunderstreak.

Nearly 4,500 F-84s were built. They were used by a good portion of the free world's air forces.

In addition to the valuable service the F-84 provided during the Korean War, the plane was involved in the development of in-flight refueling techniques for fighters. It was also the first single-seat fighter-bomber capable of carrying nuclear weapons.

Other Data (Model: F-84G)
Wingspan: 36 ft., 5 in.
Length: 38 ft., 1 in.
Power Plant: One 5,600-lb.-thrust General
    Motors turbojet
Loaded Weight: 23,525 lb.
Maximum Speed: 622 mph at sea level

Faster than the F-80 and able to carry a heavier bombload, the Thunderjet was the workhorse plane of the Korean War.

The F-86 Sabre was the Air Force's No. 1 fighter of the 1950s.

NORTH AMERICAN F-86 SABRE

The F-86 Sabre was the Air Force's first swept-wing fighter. Faster than its predecessors, the F-80 and F-84, and almost as maneuverable as a bumble-bee, the Sabre was the first American plane that could handle the Soviet MiG-15 on an equal basis.

Work on the F-86 began during the closing stages of World War II, with American designers benefiting from research that had been done by the Germans on swept-wing aircraft. An experimental model of the plane, the XP-86, first flew on November 27, 1946.

Two years later, during a shallow dive, the XP-86 became the first U.S. fighter to exceed the speed of sound, or Mach 1. (The speed of sound

38

can be from 660 mph to 790 mph, depending on altitude and temperature. Because of these variables, a plane's speed is expressed by a "Mach" number, which is the ratio of the speed of the airplane to the speed of sound in the surrounding atmosphere. A plane at Mach 1 is traveling at the speed of sound, no matter its altitude or the temperature. Mach 2 is twice the speed of sound. Mach .75 is three-fourths the speed of sound.)

In 1949, the Sabre established an air speed record of 671 mph. In 1952, another Sabre boosted the record to 698.5 mph. Still later, a third Sabre was flown at 715.7 mph.

The F-86 arrived in Korea in 1953. One U.S. pilot described the plane in these words: "As I looked out of the cockpit, the swept-back wings gave me a feeling of riding well forward on a speeding dart. Visibility was outstanding . . .

"Combat maneuvering was superb. The Sabre excelled or equalled the MiG-15 in all aspects except for service ceiling. The MiG could climb higher and in some cases faster than the Sabre, but it was no match for the F-86 below 40,000 feet."

Air Force records show that of the 839 MiGs destroyed in combat in Korea, 800 were shot down by Sabres. Only fifty-eight F-86s were lost in action.

In total, 9,502 Sabres were produced, a greater number than any aircraft since World War II. The plane served not only as the frontline fighter for the U.S. Air Force, but also for Great Britain's Royal Air Force and the air forces of Canada, Australia, Italy, and Japan. The U.S. took delivery of its last Sabre in 1956.

Other Data (Model: F-86H)
Wingspan: 37 ft., 1 in.
Length: 38 ft., 8 in.
Power Plant: One 9,000-lb.-thrust General Electric turbojet
Loaded Weight: 20,000 lb.
Maximum Speed: Over 680 mph

In total, 9,502 Sabres were produced, a greater number than any other post-World War II aircraft.

NORTH AMERICAN F-100 SUPER SABRE

The F-100 Super Sabre ushered in an era of supersonic combat equipment. While the F-86 and other early swept-wing aircraft could dive at speeds higher than Mach 1, the F-100 was the first Air Force plane to be able to achieve supersonic speeds in level flight or while climbing.

The Super Sabre came into existence as a result of Air Force demands for a fighter that would be clearly superior to Soviet-built aircraft. North American's first designs for such a plane were based on studies of the F-86D. The plane that evolved was known as the Sabre 45, because the sweep-angle of its wings was 45 degrees (as compared to a 35-degree sweep for the F-86).

While the final version of the F-100, or "Hun," as it was nicknamed by pilots of the day, generally resembled the F-86 in appearance, the new plane had several major differences. Powered by a new Pratt & Whitney J57 turbojet engine, the F-100 could develop nearly three times the thrust available to the F-86.

The F-100 had an oval air intake (the F-86's was circular) and a single-piece clamshell canopy. Its heavier armament consisted of four forward-

The F-100 Super Sabre was first Air Force fighter capable of exceeding the speed of sound in level flight.

The F-100 had distinctive oval air intake and single-piece clamshell canopy.

firing 20-mm cannons, plus two Sidewinder Bullpup AAMs (air-to-air missiles).

The Super Sabre signaled that the day of the "little" fighter had ended. Even though the F-100 was a single-seater, the plane, at 21,000 pounds, outweighed the Douglas C-47 twin-engine transport by a couple of tons.

The first of two F-100 prototypes was completed on April 24, 1953. George Welch, North American's chief pilot, exceeded the speed of sound with the plane on its first flight. The F-100 established a speed record of just over 755 mph in October, 1953.

But there were problems with the Super Sabre. The plane was involved in several accidents, one of which took the life of George Welch. All Super Sabres were grounded until an investigation could be completed. The investigation resulted in structural changes in the F-100, including a lengthening of the wing and tail fin. The new model, called the F-100C, was equipped so it could be refueled in midair from a tanker.

A total of 2,294 Super Sabres was built. The plane was still in service when, in 1962, the United States began to be drawn into the war in Vietnam. In February, 1965, F-100s took part in Operation Flaming Dart, the first Air Force strike against North Vietnam. The F-100 bore the brunt of the air war in Vietnam through 1968, often providing air cover in support of ground troops.

Other Data (Model: F-100F)
Wingspan: 39 ft.
Length: 50 ft.
Power Plant: One 10,000-lb.-thrust Pratt & Whitney turbojet
Loaded Weight: 33,000 lb.
Maximum Speed: Over 1,000 mph

An F-4 Phantom II lets loose 500-pound bombs over a Nevada bombing range.

McDONNELL-DOUGLAS F-4 PHANTOM II

The Fabulous Phantom, it was often called. One of the most versatile and popular jet fighter aircraft of all time, it was also one of the most produced. Between 1953, when design work on the plane that was to become the Phantom II began, until 1979 when production ended, more than 5,100 F-4s were built.

Fifteen distinctly different design models of the Phantom II were developed during those years. They flew with the air arms of eleven nations—the United States, Great Britain, Australia, West Germany, Greece, Iran, Egypt, Japan, South Korea, Spain, and Turkey.

The F-4 began as a project of the U.S. Navy, not the Air Force. It was the Navy that selected the name Phantom II for the plane. (The Phantom I, designed and built by McDonnell Aircraft during the 1940s, the first jet-powered carrier-based plane, was no longer in service.)

Production work on the Phantom II began in 1959 and the following year the first test flights were conducted from the aircraft carrier *Independence*. The Navy began taking delivery of the plane in 1961.

42

That same year, flight tests demonstrated that the Phantom II could outperform any and all of the Air Force's fighter planes by a wide margin. As a result, the Air Force decided to order the plane. This marked the first time the Air Force had ever purchased a plane that had been designed chiefly for carrier operations.

The Air Force's Phantom II, designated the F-4C, was capable of carrying a big weapons load, including either Sparrow or Sidewinder air-to-air missiles. A second Air Force version of the Phantom II, the RF-4C, was used for photoreconnaissance.

Both the F-4C and F-4D were used extensively in Vietnam. The D models were improved with computers used in navigating and bombing. In level flight or in a dive, at night or when the skies were overcast, the computer automatically determined the bomb release point.

The F-4E was similar to the F-4D, with the exception of an improved engine and more effective radar for self-defense.

During the course of the war, some 363 F-4s were destroyed, mostly through antiaircraft fire and in air-to-air combat. F-4s accounted for 107 MiG kills.

While F-4s are no longer being produced, many hundreds are still in service. In fact, rebuilt Phantom IIs, some with model numbers as high as F-4s, are expected to be in use until the 1990s.

Other Data (Model: F-4E)
Wingspan: 38 ft., 4 in.
Length: 63 ft.
Power Plant: Two 17,900-lb.-thrust General
    Electric turbojets
Loaded Weight: 60,630 lb.
Maximum Speed: 1,500 mph (Mach 2.27) at
    40,000 ft.

The F-4 flew with the air arms of eleven nations—including that of Egypt.

LOCKHEED F-104 STARFIGHTER

The F-104 Starfighter, one of the first fighters able to fly at speeds beyond Mach 2, dates to 1951, a year that Air Force jets in action in Korea were finding it difficult to cope with Russian-built MiG-15s. There was a critical need for a much lighter and faster combat plane.

Design work on the aircraft that was eventually to become the F-104 began in November, 1952. The first two prototypes were ready for testing during February, 1954. With a speed of 1,450 mph, the plane was almost twice as fast as any other fighter then in operation.

The F-104 was introduced to the press at a Hollywood-style preview in Palmdale, California, in April, 1956. What the writers and editors saw

when the huge curtain parted was a space age-looking aircraft. It had a pencil-thin fuselage, a T-shaped tail, and an extremely short wing, spanning less than 22 feet. Someone said the F-104 was "a missile with a man in it."

The plane's main armament had been designed for supersonic combat, where there is often time for only one quick pass. It consisted of an M-61 Vulcan cannon with a series of revolving barrels. These enabled the gun to spew out 20-mm shells at the rate of one hundred per second.

The F-104A went into active service with the Air Force in January, 1958. The following year the plane set an altitude record of 103,389 feet. But during this period, the Starfighter was plagued with accidents, and for a time all A and B models were grounded.

44

The majority of Starfighters was used by foreign nations. Germany signed a contract with Lockheed for the production of F-104Gs in that country. Of the 922 planes built under the terms of the agreement, 604 were taken by Germany, 95 by the Netherlands, 99 by Belgium, and 124 by Italy.

In the years that followed, Canada, Denmark, Greece, Japan, Jordan, Norway, Pakistan, Spain, Taiwan, and Turkey also acquired Starfighters. The plane remained in service with the U.S. Air Force until January, 1974, but many other countries continued to use the F-104 throughout the 1970s and deep into the 1980s.

Other Data (Model: F-104G)
Wingspan: 21 ft., 11 in.
Length: 54 ft., 9 in.
Power Plant: One 15,000-lb.-thrust General
   Electric turbojet
Loaded Weight: 28,779 lb.
Maximum Speed: 1,450 mph (Mach 2.2)

F-104s maneuver in the sky over San Francisco Bay.

REPUBLIC F-105 THUNDERCHIEF

For some time after it was introduced, pilots tended to look upon the F-105 Thunderchief as a mistake. The largest single-seat, single-engine aircraft ever built, the F-105 seemed too big to be able to fly well.

It was close to 70 feet in length, more than twenty feet longer than the F-100 Super Sabre. And it was, at 54,000 pounds, about twice the weight of such noted fighters as the F-86 Sabre and F-84 Thunderjet.

Pilots gave uncomplimentary names to the F-105. They called it the "Lead Sled," "Squat Bomber," "Hyper Hog," or simply "Thud."

There were also problems with the plane's

sophisticated electronics systems. At one time, it seemed there were more Thunderchiefs in shops for repair than were flying.

The role of the F-105 was to race in over an industrial target while no more than one hundred feet from the ground, drop its bombload, and then sprint away from the explosion, hitting Mach 2 in the process.

Not only was the F-105 very fast, it was also incredibly strong. The plane was built to withstand tremendous "g" forces—8 gs, in fact, or eight times the force of gravity. And it could do 1,480 mph.

An experimental Thunderchief—the YF-105A—was first flown in 1955. In the years that followed, about 75 F-105Bs and 600 F-105Ds were built. When production of the plane ended in 1965, some 900 F-105s of various models had been turned out.

Many of these planes were pressed into action in Vietnam. There the F-105 quickly proved it was no mistake. It came to be recognized as the outstanding fighter-bomber of the war, carrying out 75 percent of the tactical air strikes north of the DMZ (demilitarized zone).

One Air Force officer described the F-105's performance in these terms: "There were other aircraft carrying other loads and performing other functions, but it was the old Thud that day after day, everyday, plunged into that mess, outdueled the opposition, put the bombs on target, and dashed back to strike again."

In skies over Vietnam, F-105 Thunderchief won praise as outstanding fighter-bomber of the war.

Through the 1970s and into the 1980s, F-105s remained active, many of them seeing service with the Air National Guard and U.S. Air Force Reserve units.

Other Data (Model: F-105G)
Wingspan: 34 ft., 11 in.
Length: 69 ft., 7½ in.
Power Plant: One 24,500-lb.-thrust Pratt & Whitney turbojet
Loaded Weight: 54,000 lb.
Maximum Speed: 1,480 mph (Mach 2.25)

GENERAL DYNAMICS F-106 DELTA DART

The F-106 Delta Dart was designed as an interceptor, a plane that was to stand ready against the threat of enemy bombers. Later the plane's role was expanded to include air-to-air combat against other fighters.

How well was the F-106 expected to carry out these assignments? During most of the 1960s and on into the 1970s, North American Air Defense rested mainly with the F-106.

The F-106, called the "Six" by pilots, was a sleek beauty. It had a long needle nose, a slim and curved fuselage, an elegant delta wing, and a vertical tail fin with a rakish slant. It gave the appearance of flying even when standing silently on the runway.

From a distance, the plane's sleekness masked its size. At 70 feet, the F-106 was longer than the C-47, the famed World War II twin-engine transport. The F-106 also outweighed the C-47. But its powerful Pratt & Whitney J-75 engine could lift the F-106 to an altitude of 40,000 feet in minutes.

With its two 360-gallon wing tanks, the F-106 has a range of more than 1,500 miles. It was no problem for the plane to leave a West Coast base and cross the United States with only one refueling stop. When air refueling was used, the F-106 could span the Atlantic Ocean.

Elegant delta wing is main feature of the F-106.

The Delta Dart pilot had a choice of several tactical and defensive weapons. These included the Superfalcon air-to-air missile and the Genie air-to-air rocket with its nuclear warhead. Missiles were carried in the plane's weapons bay and were thus exposed only at the moment of launch.

The Delta Dart was first flown on December 26, 1956. Deliveries of the F-106A began three years later. A two-seat version of aircraft, called the F-106B, was also ordered by the Air Force for use as a trainer.

"After 600 hours on the F-106, I still get a thrill walking up to her side," one pilot said. "Airborne, she's a thing of beauty and a thrill to fly."

Other Data (Model: F-106A)
Wingspan: 38 ft., 3½ in.
Length: 70 ft., 8¾ in.
Power Plant: One 24,500-lb.-thrust Pratt & Whitney turbojet
Loaded Weight: 38,350 lb.
Maximum Speed: 1,525 mph (Mach 2.31)

Speeds exceeding Mach 2 were no problem for the powerful Dart.

Wing pylons enable F-111 to carry bombs, missiles, or both.

GENERAL DYNAMICS F-111

The F-111, one of the world's most advanced aircraft, is usually looked upon as a fighter. But it can also be classified as an attack bomber or a strategic bomber. Whatever you call it, the plane packs enormous punch.

The F-111's wing is fitted with eight pylons that can tote slightly more than 31,000 pounds of bombs, air-to-air missiles, or CBUs (chemical-biological units). There's also an internal weapons bay for a 20-mm rotary-barrel cannon or two additional 750-pound bombs.

What makes the F-111 futuristic is its variable-swept wings, a concept developed by Dr. Barnes Wallis, a British inventor. The wings rotate on pivots, permitting the pilot to actually redesign the shape of the aircraft in flight. On takeoffs and landings, the wings are fully extended to provide the biggest possible surface for greater lift. Relatively short takeoffs and landings are thus possible.

Once the plane is airborne and speed increases, the wing surface is then reduced by sweeping the wings back so they are tucked against the tail.

Tremendous speeds are possible when the wings are swept all the way back. The plane's announced speed is about 1,450 mph (Mach 2.2) at 30,000 feet. But one pilot has said this: "I'm not sure if anyone knows what the F-111's top speed really is. On my first flight in the F-111 we reached Mach 2 while climbing from takeoff, still relatively heavy, and had to reduce speed to keep from running out of supersonic corridor."

The F-111 also has great range. The plane has crossed the Atlantic Ocean nonstop on its internal fuel, that is, with no in-flight refueling.

The prototype of the F-111 flew on December 21, 1964. Production problems caused delays in delivering the plane, which did not go into service until 1967.

The F-111 was hailed for its performance in Vietnam, where it was used for night and all-weather attacks against the enemy. In spite of problems associated with the plane and its radar and electronics, F-111s flew nearly 3,000 missions before peace talks ended the war in 1973.

The F-111 has sometimes been the center of dispute. Some controversy has been political in nature. Some has had to do with the technical aspects of the plane. But the F-111's combat performance was never questioned. Indeed, the highest praise for the F-111 came from enemy forces.

Other Data (Model: F-111F)

Wingspan: Swept-back, 31 ft., 11.5 in.
Extended, 63 ft.
Length: 73 ft., 6 in.
Power Plant: Two 25,000-lb.-thrust Pratt & Whitney 100s
Loaded Weight: 99,000 lb.
Maximum Speed: 1,450 mph (Mach 2.2) at 35,000 ft. or above

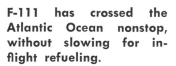

F-111 has crossed the Atlantic Ocean nonstop, without slowing for in-flight refueling.

For its effectiveness in knocking out tanks, the A-10 Thunderbolt was nicknamed the "flying can opener."

FAIRCHILD REPUBLIC A-10

During the late 1960s, the Air Force began to look for a plane that would be able to provide close support for ground troops and withstand severe damage from enemy fire. Such piston-engine planes as the F-51 Mustang, the F-82 Twin Mustang, and the Navy's Douglas A-1 Skyraider had been filling these roles.

Two planes were developed that seemed to provide what was needed—the Northrup A-9 and the Fairchild-Republic A-10. In a "fly-off" competition between the two planes held in 1972, the A-10 Thunderbolt II won. The first production A-10 was test-flown on October 21, 1975.

The A-10 was the first Air Force plane designed to deliver aerial firepower for the specific purpose of wiping out an enemy ground threat. Powered by two General Electric turbofan engines, the A-10 is able to stay within a battle zone, while packing a 9,540-pound bombload.

But the plane's most noted feature is its 30-mm, seven-barrel, tank-busting gun, the most powerful gun of its type ever built. It delivers twenty times the muzzle power of the 75-mm antitank gun used in World War II.

Known as the GAU-8/A, but nicknamed the "Avenger," the gun is mounted internally along the plane's centerline. It is capable of firing at a speed of either 2,100 or 4,200 rounds-per-minute. Besides the armor-piercing projectiles the "Avenger" fires, which are capable of penetrating the outer shell of both medium and heavy tanks, the gun can also handle high-explosive ammunition, which is effective against many different types of vehicles.

At Nellis Air Force base in Nevada, the A-10 demonstrated its tank-killing ability by knocking out test tanks with one- and two-second bursts from the "Avenger." Little wonder the plane is sometimes referred to as the "flying can opener."

The A-10 is also one of the most indestructible of all aircraft. It is said it can lose one engine, half a tail, two-thirds of the wing, and parts of the fuselage—and still remain airborne.

Other Data (Model: A-10A)
Wingspan: 57 ft., 6 in.
Length: 43 ft., 4 in.
Power Plant: Two 9,065-lb.-thrust General
    Electric turbojets
Loaded Weight: 22,844 lb.
Maximum Speed: 448 mph at 10,000 ft.

In demonstration of its short takeoff and landing capability, an A-10 uses a highway as airstrip.

During mid-1970s, the F-15 took over as the Air Force's No. 1 fighting plane.

McDONNELL-DOUGLAS F-15 EAGLE

During the decade of the 1980s, the twin-engine F-15 Eagle ranked as the U.S. Air Force's best operational fighter. To some observers, it was the world's best.

With its Mach 2.5 speed, the F-15 provides the Air Force with the ability to intercept and destroy any enemy aircrift in any weather, day or night.

The typical F-15 armament consists of four radar-guided Sparrow air-to-air missiles and four infrared-guided Sidewinder missiles · or eight medium-range air-to-air missiles, plus a 20-mm Gatling gun with 940 rounds of ammunition. The plane also boasts the most up-to-date radar and electronic countermeasure systems.

The first flight of the F-15 took place on July 27, 1972, at Edwards Air Force Base, California. The first two production aircraft were delivered to the Air Force on November 14, 1974.

The F-15 is approximately the same size as its older cousin, McDonnell-Douglas' F-4 Phantom II. However, the F-15's takeoff weight is about 6,000 pounds less than that of the F-4.

The F-15 is powered by two Pratt & Whitney F100 turbofans. They deliver tremendous thrust. Once, a specially prepared Eagle, nicknamed the "Streak Eagle," took part in a test flight in which the aircraft ran up its engines while parked on the runway, then shot up rocketlike to over 39,000 feet

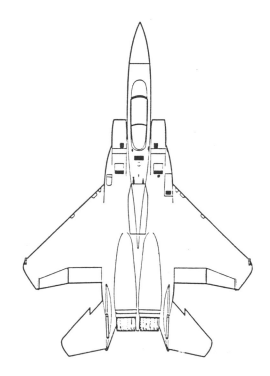

The F-15 Eagle has modified delta wing.

in less than one minute. It didn't stop climbing until it had reached 103,000 feet. At one time, the F-15 held eight time-to-climb records.

Mechanics praise the Eagle as much as pilots do. The plane doesn't require nearly as much maintenance as the F-4. There is easy access to the various engine components. The engine itself can be removed in twenty minutes or even less. Many

55

of the plane's electronic devices have their own built-in test systems.

The Eagle has demonstrated its all-weather capability by foiling F-4s and F-111s in NATO exercises. Flying in the worst of weather, a single F-15 intercepted two F-111s approaching Great Britain from the north. The plane's radar detected the first of the "enemy" aircraft at a range of one hundred miles. The F-15 was then directed against a third F-111 flying at low altitude, and this threat was also intercepted and "destroyed."

Another exercise matched an Eagle on air combat patrol at 15,000 feet against a pair of F-4 Phantoms flying at altitudes of between 500 and 800 feet. Not only did the F-15 "destroy" both of the "enemy" aircraft, but in each case it did so in a single pass.

It's not just in mock war "games" that the F-15 has distinguished itself. In June, 1979, American-supplied F-15s flown by Israeli pilots clashed with Syrian Air Force MiG-21s over southern Lebanon. It was the first time in history that *advanced* U.S.

Typical F-15 armament consists of both Sparrow and Sidewinder air-to-air missiles.

At one time, the F-15 held eight "time-to-climb" records.

jets had been used in combat. Israel said its pilots shot down at least five Syrian aircraft. All Israeli planes returned safely to their base.

During the early 1980s, F-15As and F-15Bs were replaced by F-15Cs (single-seat) and F-15Ds (two-seat). These models had electronics systems that enabled the pilot to continue tracking one target while searching for others.

During the late 1980s, the Air Force began taking delivery of the F-15E, a dual-role fighter. It has a capability of performing long-range air-to-ground missions, even at night and in bad weather. The plane also rates, of course, as a superior air-to-air fighting machine.

The F-15 serves with the U.S. Air Force in the continental United States, Alaska, in Europe and the Pacific. It not only flies with the Israeli Air Force, but also with the Japanese Self-Defense Air Force. If the United States is ever threatened from the air, the F-15 is likely to be the first plane to answer that threat.

Other Data (Model: F-15A)
Wingspan: 42 ft., 9 in.
Length: 63 ft., 9 in.
Power Plant: Two 25,000-lb.-thrust Pratt & Whitney turbofans
Loeded Weight: 40,000 lb.
Maximum Speed: 1,650 mph (Mach 2.5) at 36,000 ft.

The F-16 Fighting Falcon has excellent speed, great range, and is exceptionally maneuverable.

GENERAL DYNAMICS F-16

"There is, in my mind, simply no other plane in the world today that I would rather take into combat, if it became necessary." That's how Capt. Wayne C. Edwards, an F-16 instructor-pilot, writing in *Air Force Magazine*, spoke of this ship. "This is the plane I want to be teamed with for the rest of my flying days," Captain Edwards added.

Such praise is not unusual for the F-16 Fighting Falcon. The most maneuverable fighter in the world, the Falcon has also been hailed for its excellent speed, exceptional range, and superior weapons system.

The F-16 was planned as a new concept in fighter aircraft. From the time of the F-86 Sabre to the F-15 Eagle, one plane after the next was able to fly higher, faster, and farther than the plane that preceded it.

But to provide for this greater capability, fighters kept becoming bigger, heavier, and more complex —and more costly. The F-16 interrupted the trend. It packed its tremendous speed, range, and firepower into a relatively small airframe.

A test model of the F-16, the YF-16, was first flown in February, 1974. Less than a year later, the U.S. Air Force announced that it was ordering 650 F-16s. The first operational F-16s were delivered to Hill Air Force Base, Utah, in 1979.

From the beginning, the F-16 earned high marks for safety. In fact, it compiled the best safety record of any single-engine fighter in Air Force history. In 1983, the Air Force had its safest flying year ever. The F-16's low accident rate was a major factor in the achievement of that record.

The F-16 has nine stations for carrying weapons —six under the wings, two on the wing tips, and one on the fuselage centerline. These stations can be fitted with missile launchers that enable the plane to carry the latest in laser- and television-guided air-to-air or air-to-surface munitions. The stations can also accommodate bomb racks for carrying free-fall bombs. In addition, the F-16's armament includes a 20-mm multibarrel cannon.

By changing the array of weapons that the F-16 carries, the role of the plane can be modified. The Fighting Falcon can be used to establish superiority in the air through the use of air-to-air missiles, or it can be used to take the fight to the enemy by attacking ground targets, when equipped with air-to-surface missiles.

In 1983, the U.S. Air Force's Air Demonstration Squadron, popularly known as the Thunderbirds, began flying F-16s. Previously the Thunderbirds had flown the Northrop T-38 Talon, a training plane for supersonic flight, and before that the F-4, F-105, F-100, and F-84. The Thunderbirds were founded in 1953.

During the 1983 season, the Thunderbirds per-

F-16, on a training mission, prepares to launch one of its Sidewinder air-to-air missiles.

An F-16 banks over the Nevada desert not far from Nellis Air Force Base.

formed 78 shows for more than 16 million people in the United States.

The F-16, with its greater range, gave the Thunderbirds the capability of performing overseas, which was not possible with the T-38. During 1984, the Thunderbirds performed their aerobatics for enthusiastic audiences in Western Europe and Africa.

One of the Air Force's principal fighters of the 1990s is likely to be the F-16F, which was flying as early as 1982 as the F-16XL. The F-16F's most startling innovation is a new wing, a wing with more than twice the area of the standard F-16 wing. Called a "cranked arrow" wing, it was de-

veloped by General Dynamics in close cooperation with the Langley Research Center, a division of the National Aeronautics and Space Administration.

The wing is covered with a graphite skin for greater strength and lower weight. It enables the plane to carry about 1,100 more pounds of fuel, thus increasing the plane's range without need for external fuel tanks.

The F-16F is a slightly bigger plane than the earlier model Falcon. It is 54.2 feet in length and has a 34.2-foot wingspan. It is powered by an advanced version of the Pratt & Whitney F100 or General Electric F110 engine.

In recent years, the F-16 has won wide acceptance internationally. It was chosen by four nations of the North Atlantic Treaty Organization (NATO) —Belgium, Denmark, Holland, and Norway—to replace their aging F-104s. Those nations have also shared in the manufacture of the F-116. Assembly lines are in operation not only at the General Dynamics plant at Fort Worth, Texas, but also in Gosselies, Belgium, and near Amsterdam, Holland.

Israel has acquired the plane for its air force and the plane has also been ordered by Egypt, South Korea, Pakistan, Venezuela, and Turkey.

By the mid-1980s, more than 1,200 F-16s were in use by the U.S. Air Force and the air forces of its allies. It was being called the most sought-after fighter in the free world.

Latest version of Fighting Falcon is the F-16F.

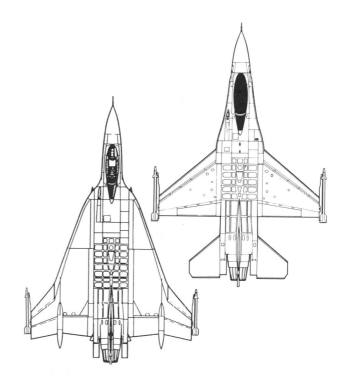

F-16F (left) is slightly larger than F-16A and has "cranked arrow" wing.

Other Data (Model: F-16A)
Wingspan: 31 ft.
Length: 47 ft., 7¾ in.
Power Plant: One 25,000-lb.-thrust Pratt & Whitney turbofan
Loaded Weight: 24,460
Maximum Speed: 1,255 mph (Mach 1.95) at 36,000 ft.

STEALTH FIGHTER

As early as 1962, reports began to be heard about a project to develop an aircraft that would be invisible to radar. Stories about such a plane appeared in such publications as *Defense Daily* and *Aerospace Daily* in 1975.

Then in 1980, *Armed Forces Journal* disclosed that the United States had been flying a "virtually invisible aircraft" for two years. Not long after the article appeared, Harold Brown, Secretary of Defense under President Jimmy Carter, confirmed that the United States had, indeed, test-flown a plane that was hard for radar to detect. Brown declared that it "cannot be successfully intercepted with existing air defense systems." He also boasted that the development "alters the military balance in favor of the United States."

"Stealth" is the popular word used to describe the technology that renders an airplane virtually invisible to radar. It means secret or furtive.

The Northrop Corporation began developing a Stealth bomber, or Advanced Technology Bomber (ATB), in the late 1970s. The Stealth fighter is a project of the Lockheed-California Corporation.

Lockheed is said to have produced three proto-type Stealth fighters by the early 1980s. Flying from secret airfields, including Eielson Air Force Base, Alaska, and one near Groom Lake, Nevada, two of the triangular-shaped craft crashed. A third continued to fly.

Little was known by the public about the design of the Stealth fighter at the time this chapter was being written, except that its engines blended with its wing to eliminate the flat planes and sharp corners that reflect radar.

The fighter was believed to have been made chiefly of Fibaloy, a synthetic material developed by the Dow Chemical Company. Fibaloy consists of glass fibers embedded in plastic. Not only is Fibaloy strong enough to form the aircraft's skin and main structural parts, but it also absorbs and deflects radar signals.

Lightweight is another feature of Fibaloy. The Stealth fighter is light enough—and small enough—to be carried inside a C-5A transport.

The Stealth fighter benefits from Lockheed's experience with the SR-71 Blackbird, a spy plane. The Blackbird got its name from its inky-black coating, which reduced its radar "signature" and served to camouflage the aircraft against the dark sky.

Stealth fighter will offer characteristics similar to Lockheed's sophisticated SR-71, a reconnaissance aircraft.

FAMOUS AIRCRAFT ON DISPLAY

Most of the aircraft featured in this book (and other books of the series) can be seen, studied, and photographed at the various air museums to be found throughout the United States. Even such planes as historic as the Curtiss JN-4, as famous as the North American P-51 Mustang, as significant as the Lockheed XP-80 Shooting Star, and as big as the Boeing B-17 Flying Fortress are on exhibition.

These display facilities include:

• Ames-Dryden Flight Research Facility, National Aeronautics and Space Administration (P.O. Box 273, Edwards, CA 93523); mostly NASA aircraft, such as the B-52 used to drop the X-15.

• Florence Air and Missile Museum (P.O. Box 1326, Florence, SC 29503); 38 aircraft, including jet fighters and bombers.

• National Air and Space Museum (Smithsonian Institution, Washington DC 20560); more than 275 aircraft, probably the best collection in the world.

• Naval Air Test & Evaluation Museum (P.O. Box 407, Naval Air Test Center, Patuxent River, MD 20670).

• Naval Aviation Museum (Pensacola, FL 32508).

• New England Air Museum (Bradley International Airport, Windsor Locks, CT 06096); comprehensive, impressive collection of about 100 aircraft.

• Pate Museum of Transportation (P.O. Box 711, Fort Worth, TX 76101).

• Pima Air Museum (6400 S. Wilmot, Tucson, AZ 85706); the third largest collection of historic aircraft in the U.S.

• San Diego Aerospace Museum (2001 Pan American Plaza, Balboa Park, San Diego, CA 92101); a journey through the history of flight; extensive, varied collection.

• U.S. Air Force Museum (Wright-Patterson Air Force Base, Dayton, OH 45433); the oldest and biggest aviation museum in the world.

• U.S. Army Aviation Museum (Fort Rucker, AL 36362); the largest collection of helicopters in the world.

• U.S. Marine Corps Aviation Museum (Brown Field, Quantico, VA 22134); Marine Corps historic aircraft beginning with World War I).

Write the museums for more information, including viewing hours and possible admission fees. Be aware that many aircraft are in outdoor storage, and thus can be viewed only when weather conditions permit.